Contents

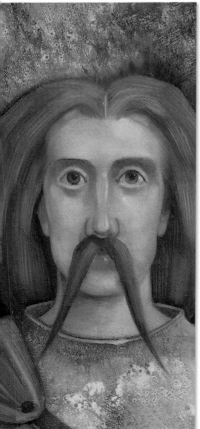

ORIGINS OF THE ANCIENT CELTS

THE ORIGINAL HOME OF THE CELTS, ALSO KNOWN as Kelts, is shrouded in mystery. Ancient writers knew so little about them they were called the "people who came out of the darkness." The Greeks referred to them as **Keltoi.** The Romans translated the word into Latin—**Celtae**—and also called them Gauls, or "strangers." Many modern scholars use the names "Celts" or "Gauls" interchangeably.

The earliest knowledge we have of the Celts doesn't come from them. Their culture was **preliterate**, which means they had no written language. Scholars have collected information about the Celts from letters, documents, and journals written by Greek and Roman officials, geographers, and historians.

Around 500 B.C., early writers noted that the Celts lived near the important trade center of Massilia, which is the site of modern-day Marseille, France.

A later painting imagines Gauls guarding the coast of what is now France.

The Greek historian Herodotus (c. 484–c. 425 B.C.) reported Celts also dwelled "beyond the pillars of Hercules," an area known today as the Straits of Gibraltar. Other sources include the writings of Rome's first emperor, Julius Caesar (100-44 B.C.), the Greek geographer Strabo (c. 64 B.C.–c. A.D.21), and the Roman historian Livy (59 B.C.–A.D. 17).

United by Speech

The Celts weren't a single large tribe but many separate tribes linked by similar traditions and a lifestyle based on farming and cattle raising. Most importantly, they were connected by a set of related languages. Linguists (scholars who study language) believe Celtic languages evolved from the Indo-European tongue, which originated in Asia about 4000 B.C. Between 1300 and 800 B.C. the Italic, Slavic, and Germanic languages also developed from this source.

In the second century B.C., the Greek historian Polybius noted "where the Po River rises [lived] the Laii and Libici; beyond them the Insubres, the largest of the Celtic tribes . . . land south of the Po was settled by the Anari, east of them the Boii, towards the Adriatic the Lingones . . . on the coast, the Senones." Strabo added sixty other names to the list, among them the Helvetii, Vivisci, and Arverni.

Europe's First Horsemen

Archaeological evidence indicates horses were hunted in prehistoric times for meat, as were other large animals. When horses were domesticated on the steppes of Asia in about 4000 B.C., they were used as pack animals. Eventually, people began to ride them. Horses were introduced to western Europe around 3000 B.C.

Fiercely Loyal

Although they shared similar languages and lifestyles, Celtic tribes didn't unite under the flag of a single king. No matter its size, each tribe was fiercely loyal to its own warlord. Historians agree that if the Celts had banded together, they might have successfully resisted the Roman armies.

During their time, the Celts were skilled horsemen. On horseback the Celts, who were always in search of better farmland, roamed farther than before. They became warlike marauders, spilling blood and seizing the property of others.

The Greek historian Diodorus Siculus, writing between 60 B.C. and 30 B.C., painted a frightening portrait of Celtic warriors: "tall of body, with rippling muscles, and white of skin," resembling "wood demons, their hair thick and shaggy like a horse's mane." Celtic women, said to be equally impressive, went into battle beside their husbands and brothers.

A Celtic coin features a horse and rider. The Celts were known as expert horsemen.

Wild Beasts

The established Greek and Roman civilizations enjoyed the advantages of walled cities and rule of law. The barbarians, including not only Celts but also Scythians, Persians, and Libyans, hadn't achieved such levels of security. Yet it was the Celts—"wild beasts whose blood we must shed or spill our own," said Livy—who were feared most because they roamed freely from the Black Sea in the east and to what is now Spain and Portugal in the west.

The Celts' warlike behavior disturbed the rulers of Greece and Rome, yet the rulers were confident the icy walls of the Alps provided a natural barrier against invasion. The frozen mountains might have kept the Celts out of the Mediterranean if not for two common minerals: iron and salt.

People of Iron

About 1300 B.C., the Hittites (of modern Turkey) discovered when certain rust-colored rocks were heated to 3,400 degrees Fahrenheit (1,871 degrees Celsius), a metal harder than bronze (a mixture

The ancient Greeks and Romans believed that the Alps would provide enough of a barrier to protect them from the Celts.

Celtic Vanity

Celtic warriors were proud of their tall, strong bodies. They were weight-conscious, too, and ridiculed men who sported pot bellies. They enhanced the color of their reddish-blond hair by bleaching it in lime water, which made it coarse and thick. Their moustaches grew so long over their mouths that they acted like sieves, trapping particles of food.

The Celts thrived during the Iron Age. This is a recreation of a dwelling from that time period.

of copper and tin) was produced. The Greeks learned how to process iron ore, too. The craft spread into Europe, where the Celts also mastered the production of slab iron.

Between 750 and 500 B.C., the Celts settled in permanent communities near large deposits of iron ore. They made swords, spears, and daggers that could be honed (sharpened) to keener edges than could bronze weapons. Iron plows, saws, and axes were longer wearing. The Celts also fashioned jewelry—rings, bracelets, buckles, brooches—out of iron, earning them the name "People of Iron."

After settling at Hallstatt, which is located in what is now Austria, where there were deposits of salt as well as iron, the Celts began to trade extensively with the Mediterranean empires. Traders returned with tales of the sunny, fertile fields of northern Italy; soon the temptation to seize them became irresistible. Around 400 B.C., Celts braved the icy slopes of the Alps and poured into the Po Valley, for as the historian J. A. Mauduit noted, the Celts were "the most adventurous of all the barbarian peoples." They drove out local farmers and seized their fields for themselves.

Two Important Discoveries: Hallstatt and La Tène

In 1846, the Austrian government reopened an old salt mine at the foot of Salzburg ("salt mountain") near the village of Hallstatt. When a road was built to transport salt out of the region, seven skeletons were discovered. Georg Ramsauer, director of the project, believed he'd uncovered a cemetery of "heathens." Later,

"White Gold"

Tales about the Celts had been told for centuries, but no one ever found any proof of their existence. When evidence was discovered, it was linked to salt, not iron. Salt, a food preservative, was so valuable in ancient times it was called "white gold." The most important trade routes in the ancient world were the *Salzkammergut*, or "salt roads."

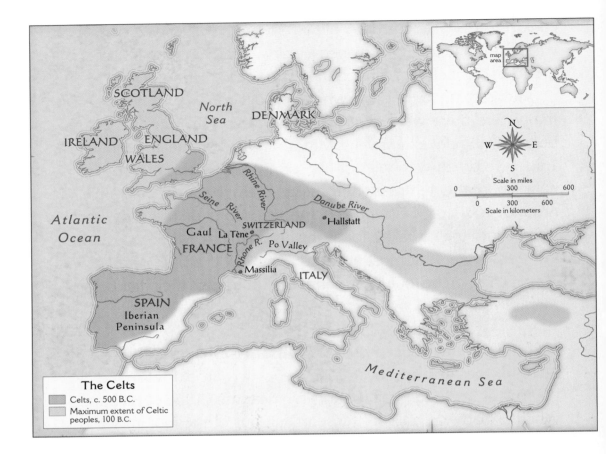

The Celts
- Celts, c. 500 B.C.
- Maximum extent of Celtic peoples, 100 B.C.

graves of 980 Celts dating from about 700 B.C. to 400 B.C. were found, as well as 6,000 artifacts, including jewelry, tools, weapons, bowls, and horse gear. Archaeologists named this the Hallstatt site.

In 1857, Friedrich Schwab, an amateur explorer, made a similar discovery. Using a homemade dredge at Lake Neuchâtel in Switzerland, Schwab recovered 3,000 Celtic artifacts, such as tools, horse gear, and more than 160 swords and iron scabbards dating from about 300 B.C. Archaeologists call this the La Tène site ("the shallows"), referring to the depth of the lake.

Archaeological Periods

Before 7000 B.C.	Old Stone Age (Paleolithic)
7000 B.C.–**4000** B.C.	Middle Stone Age (Mesolithic)
4000 B.C.–**2000** B.C.	New Stone Age (Neolithic)
2000 B.C.–**1200** B.C.	Early Bronze Age
1200 B.C.–**700** B.C.	Late Bronze Age
700 B.C.–A.D. **500**	Iron Age—Age of the Celts

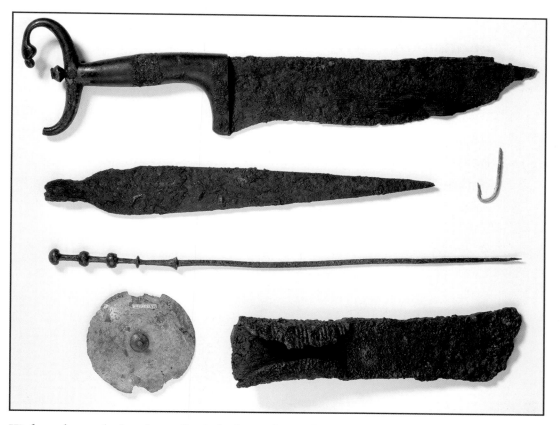

We have learned a lot about the Celts from the artifacts they left behind. These are tools and weapons made by the Celts. From top to bottom, there is a knife, a spearhead, a fish hook, a clothes pin, belt disc, and axe.

Carbon Dating

Dr. Willard F. Libby, an American chemist, received a Nobel prize in chemistry in 1960 for the discovery of a method to determine the age of ancient material that was once living. Carbon 14 (C_{14}) is constantly produced by radiation from the sun and is taken up by living things, such as humans, animals, plants, and trees. Uptake of C_{14} ceases on the death of the tissue, then decays at a predictable rate. The ratio of carbon types remaining in the tissue can be measured, determining the age of a material.

Permanent Legacy

The Celts weren't civilized in the same way as the Greeks and Romans were. Yet they were skilled craftspeople who produced tools, weapons, and ornaments in iron and bronze. They were successful farmers, wealthy in crops and cattle. They were expert horsemen, hardened in battle. When the Celts stepped out of the darkness, they left a permanent mark on the world we live in. Among their legacies was a hero for the ages: King Arthur.

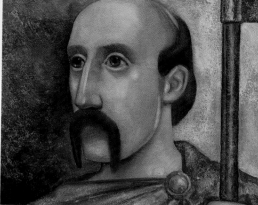

Chapter I

FARMERS, CROPS, AND LIVESTOCK

In ancient times the Celts were said to be so fond of battle they'd fight each other if they had no other enemy. Their reputation as warriors caused early historians to call them barbarians whose only interest was gaining wealth from the proceeds of war. The Celts' true wealth didn't come from battlefields, though. It came from their skills as farmers and raisers of livestock.

The Celts preferred farmland along the great rivers of Europe—the Seine, Rhone, Rhine, and Danube—where soil was most fertile. Such land often contained clay, making the soil difficult to plow. Although the Celts had farmed successfully for centuries, iron changed *how* they farmed.

After the Celts learned to smelt iron, they put iron tips on their plows, enabling them to till heavy soil more easily. Using iron scythes and sickles meant crops could be harvested faster. Iron axes helped clear forests for new cropland more efficiently. An illustration at a grave site in France indicates the Celts even invented a reaper, further increasing their

While the Celts were often thought of as warriors, they were also great farmers. A Celtic sculpture shows a farmer using animals to pull a plow.

productivity. Ever more cropland was needed to feed an increasing population, so the Celts pushed east into the Balkans as well as west into the Iberian Peninsula (modern Portugal and Spain).

Circle of Safety

Celtic farmers lived close to each other on 4- to 6-acre (1.6- to 2.4-hectare) plots. In Ireland in around A.D. 600, each was built inside a *rath*, a circle about 100 feet (33 meters) in diameter, barricaded at the outer edge by an earthen embankment and a deep ditch. The bank and ditch kept animal and human predators at bay. Other Celts built rectangular wooden houses and wooden and stone roundhouses.

Four generations of kin lived near each other. When a farmer looked across the countryside, he saw raths belonging to his grandfather, father, and brothers. In a world of hostile forces—enemy tribes, hungry wolves, fierce weather—it was a comforting sight. At a grandfather's death, his property was divided. The

When Plows Were Made of Wood

The discovery of an ancient settlement in Jutland (modern Denmark) indicates an **ard**, a simple wooden plow, was one of Iron Age farmers' earliest tools. The triangular plowshare broke up the ground but had no **moldboard** (curved blade) to turn the soil over. Evidence found in layers of a nearby **peat** bog indicate that farmers compensated by plowing twice: first in one direction, then crosswise at an angle to better break up the soil. This time-consuming practice kept fields small.

Based on excavations in England, a modern sketch depicts a typical Celtic village.

youngest son decided how the land would be shared—but he was the last to choose—giving him reason to be fair.

The house inside the rath was circular, too, about 20 feet (6.1 m) in diameter. The roof was made of reed thatch, the walls of **wattle** and **daub**. Wattle was made by driving poles vertically into the ground at regular intervals. Flexible tree branches such as willow were woven back and forth between the upright poles, creating a thick screen. A single opening away from the prevailing wind served as a doorway.

Clay or mud mixed with straw was daubed (smeared or patted) over the wattle screen. Moss, clay, or tree pitch was stuffed into any remaining holes. If the wall was damaged, it was easily repaired by reweaving willow branches and adding more daub.

A stone hearth in the center of the house provided heat and a place to cook. A large iron pot heated over a peat fire usually held barley porridge or a fragrant stew of beef, pork, or mutton to which onions, turnips, and wild garlic were added. Such meals were eaten from wooden bowls. As darkness fell, the room was lighted by candles made of beef tallow or beeswax.

Warm and Weatherproof

In 1976, researchers at the Butser Ancient Farm research center at Hampshire, England, constructed a prehistoric Celtic roundhouse. Oak posts were set vertically, flexible tree branches were woven between them, then daub was mixed of clay, straw, and animal hair. The roof was thatched with straw. When finished, the dwelling proved to be warm and weatherproof in winter.

The hearth in the middle of the farmhouse provided heat as well as a cooking area.

At bedtime family members slept on beds made of wooden planks covered with barley or wheat straw. Wicker screens provided a bit of privacy. A leather rug or two might cover the dirt floor. The discovery of Iron Age homes in Poland dating from 550 B.C. indicates that floors also were covered with several layers of leafy twigs.

People and Animals Side by Side

Iron Age farmers at Grontoft, a village dating from 500 B.C. in Denmark, built longhouses rather than circular ones. People lived in the smaller half of the house; the larger half was divided into stalls for horses and cattle. A household's wealth could be determined by the number of stalls: eight to eighteen for successful farmers, three or four for those less well off. The poorest farmers had none and probably exchanged their labor with neighbors for milk, butter, and cheese.

Celtic Fields and Fences

Farm fields were marked off by stone walls or fences woven of thorny branches to keep cattle, sheep, and pigs from damaging crops. On May 1, animals were driven out to open pasture (the Irish Celts called it **booleying**) so they wouldn't trample the newly planted fields. In autumn, the animals were brought back and led into the harvested fields to feast on husks. Their droppings provided fertilizer for next season's crops.

Farmers who lived near the seacoast, as did the Celts of Ireland, Scotland, and Britain, also used seaweed as fertilizer. Before new fields were plowed, **turf** was burned to make plowing easier, and the ash added nutrients to the soil. Plowing usually began in March as soon as the soil was dry. It was a cooperative effort, for families couldn't afford to own all the necessary equipment—oxen, harnesses, a plow. They pooled their resources and shared their labor.

Not all farmers owned their lands. In Ireland during the Early Medieval period, a **freeman** was a tenant farmer who had a seven-year contract with a noble. The noble rented seven cows and a bull, a sow and seven piglets, seven sheep, and one horse to the freeman, plus land on which to graze them. Once a year the freeman paid the noble with a finished product. For example, he paid in beer, not in the barley used to make the beer. At the end of seven years, the rented animals became the property of the freeman. He could enter into another contract with the noble or seek a better one with a different noble.

The Celts' Most Valuable Livestock

Prehistoric humankind depended on hunters to provide meat to feed a tribe. If hunting was poor, people went hungry. When agriculture and the domestication of animals evolved, life became easier. Livestock could be kept close by and slaughtered when meat was needed.

The most important animals among Celtic farmers were cattle, but not merely for their meat. From cows came milk, butter,

A Farmer's Calendar

A farmer's year was divided into four parts, each celebrated with a festival. **Imbolc**, February 1, marked the beginning of spring and lambing season. **Beltane**, May 1, heralded the beginning of summer and the moving of cattle and sheep to high pastures. **Lughnasadh**, August 1, signaled the beginning of the autumn harvest. **Samhain** (we call it Halloween) began on October 31 or November 1 and celebrated the beginning of winter.

Cattle were essential for the survival of the Celts since they were a source of food and clothing. This vessel depicts a cow and its calf and was used for serving food.

and cheese. Older cows and bulls not kept for breeding were killed for food. Leather from their hides was used to make shoes, caps, belts, harnesses, and even sails for boats. Cattle were so valuable they were the object of many a **táin**, or cattle raid. Cattle rustling—considered despicable in the American West—was the subject of Celtic tales in which the thief was seen as a hero, not as a villain.

Crops Planted

Barley and millet were the first grains planted by the early Celts because they were so hardy. Oats and rye also were planted.

Wheat was the most nutritious grain, however. Modern plant scientists have determined that the types of wheat planted in ancient times—**einkorn**, **spelt**, and **emmer**—contained twice as much protein as modern varieties do.

Archaeologists have helped shed light on how the Celts stored these grains. In 1969, a hill fort at Danebury in southern England was excavated, revealing pits 3 feet (1 m) in diameter and 6 feet (2 m) deep that had been dug into the earth, filled with grain, and then sealed with clay lids that shed water. To determine the efficiency of such granaries, British archaeologists dug similar pits. Each was filled with a ton of wheat, sealed, and left for the winter. When the granary was opened in the spring, only 2 percent of the grain had spoiled.

Other important crops for the Celts included vegetables, such as onions, peas, beans, lentils, cabbage, turnips, and carrots.

Pollen, Teller of Tales

Scientists have discovered that pollen grains resist decay better than other parts of a plant do, especially if preserved in peat bogs. Oak pollen was found in the deepest (oldest) layer of peat in a third-century settlement in Bavaria, indicating the region once was covered by oak forest. Pollen from dandelions—light-loving plants—was preserved in the middle layers, suggesting the forests had been cleared for fuel and lumber. Wheat pollen found in the upper layers indicates that farmers had begun to plant fields of wheat.

Under proper conditions (cool and dry), such vegetables could be stored for a length of time. Apple trees grew wild, and their fruit was eaten by people and animals alike. Flax was an important crop because its fibers were used to make rope and were woven into linen cloth.

A Life Ruled by the Seasons

Many aspects of a farmer's life revolved around the seasons, such as what he wore and what he ate. A farmer's clothing consisted of a linen tunic that came to his knees and was cinched around his waist with a leather belt. If the weather was cold, he pulled on colorful plaid trousers and wrapped a large wool cloak (which sometimes served as a blanket) about himself, fastening it with a brooch made of iron or bronze. Women's garments were equally simple. A blouse with large sleeves was worn over a full skirt and was belted at the waist. Greek and Roman writers noted that children were dressed lightly even in winter. The Celts believed children should be taught early that life was harsh.

Hill Forts in Scotland

A Celtic hill fort near Abernethy, Scotland, enclosed about 0.125 acre (506 square meters). Archaeologists calculate that the construction of the fort's walls required 3,200 feet (975 m) of lumber; 640 trees, or about 60 acres (24 ha) of forest, had to be cut to acquire the needed lumber. Such forts are probably one reason areas of the British Isles and northern Europe lost extensive forests in ancient times.

Celts used looms to make cloth. This replica depicts the style of loom used around the eighth to third century B.C.

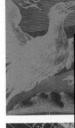

A Celt's Best Friend

The bones of several dogs were found in Flag Fen, a marsh at Cambridgeshire in Britain. Swords, spears, and pottery were discovered at the same place, thought to be a site where offerings were made to the gods. In Celtic legend dogs were gifts fit for kings. After the Romans conquered Britain in the first century A.D., one of the items they expected to be paid in tribute were fine Celtic hunting dogs.

As winter winds howled, families stayed indoors. They ate "winter food," usually salted beef or pork as well as porridge made from grains such as barley and oats. Flour could be made from stored wheat, which was "hardened" first in a kiln. A kiln was made by digging a shallow pit and lining it with stones. Grain was piled into the pit, covered by a layer of peat, then set afire. The peat burned slowly, creating an oven that dried the grain. "Summer food" consisted of a rich variety of vegetables as well as fruits, nuts, and berries gathered from meadows and woods.

Farmers' winters were a time to socialize, make arrangements with neighbors about sharing work, and forge marriage contracts between sons and daughters. Not least, it was a time to tell stories—a favorite Celtic pastime—and to enjoy drinking ale (beer made from barley) or **mead** (wine made from honey).

Chapter II

FAMILY AND SOCIETY

Greeks and Romans were surprised by the many rights Celtic women enjoyed compared to females in their own cultures. Although the philosopher Pythagoras (c. 582–507 B.C.) encouraged Greek women to become leaders, they never achieved what was taken for granted among the Celts. A Celtic woman could divorce her husband, own a business, and inherit property. She could cancel contracts made by her husband if she thought they were foolish and could take a case to court without his approval. A nobleman's wife had the right to be consulted on every subject.

A Celtic woman could marry whom she pleased if she were determined to do so. Usually, marriage was considered too important to be left solely to personal choice, because it united not merely a couple but groups of people. Marriage created social, political, and economic bonds that provided security in times of need. The threat of enemy invasion, crop failures, or losses in battle were good reasons to build extended families. Marriages among nobles as well as commoners were usually arranged by parents eager to forge connections with other tribes.

In Celtic culture, usually parents determined who their children would marry.

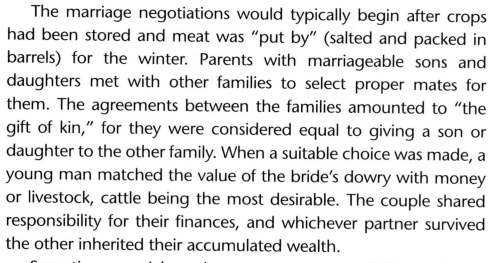

Awesome Beauty

The Roman writer Ammianus Marcellinus observed that Celtic women possessed an awesome sort of beauty. He wrote, "they went into battle with "gleaming eyes [they were] . . . more than a match for a whole group of foreigners." Ancient artwork is proof of the esteem in which Celtic women were held: They were depicted exactly the same size as men.

The marriage negotiations would typically begin after crops had been stored and meat was "put by" (salted and packed in barrels) for the winter. Parents with marriageable sons and daughters met with other families to select proper mates for them. The agreements between the families amounted to "the gift of kin," for they were considered equal to giving a son or daughter to the other family. When a suitable choice was made, a young man matched the value of the bride's dowry with money or livestock, cattle being the most desirable. The couple shared responsibility for their finances, and whichever partner survived the other inherited their accumulated wealth.

Sometimes special marriage arrangements could be made. If a couple in Celtic Ireland weren't sure they were suited to each other, they might enter a trial marriage. Their vows were valid for a year from the date they were made. At Tailtiu (modern-day Teltown, Ireland), a trial agreement commenced when a couple approached each other and exchanged kisses. A year later, the arrangement could be dissolved at the same spot by simply walking away from each other.

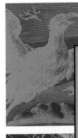

Almost Equal, but Not Quite

As equitable as Celtic marriage appeared to be, a man held the power of life and death over his wife and children. His relatives did too. According to Caesar's account of Celtic marriage, if a man died under suspicious circumstances, his relatives could use torture to force a confession from the widow. If convinced of her guilt, they could put her to death.

Other Celts could end their marriages too. Legal separation or divorce was permitted among the Celts, and each spouse was entitled to take from the marriage half the assets that had been acquired. A man could divorce a wife if she didn't bear children. A woman could divorce a husband if he got fat, for obesity was scorned. Both men and women were entitled to remarry and did, often more than once.

More Than One Wife

Monogamy was practiced by peoples of the Mediterranean, but Celtic culture permitted men to have more than one spouse. The first wife was always the "chief" wife and retained her rights of inheritance. If a husband decided to take a second wife, the first was entitled to be paid compensation in the form of money, land, or livestock. Two wives living under the same roof were apt to quarrel, so a man usually provided a house for each one. Women didn't take second husbands, however, and could be killed if they were unfaithful.

The most important obligation a woman had in marriage was to produce children. Every wife hoped to give birth to sons,

The Celts believed that it was important to have children. The remains of a
Celtic sculpture depicts parents with their child.

although girls were valuable, because they could be married to
the sons of other tribes. Celtic children didn't go to school as we
think of it. Farmers' sons worked in the fields as soon as they were
able, and daughters in the home, while the offspring of nobles
were educated to become rulers.

Fosterage: Building Bonds

In addition to marriage, **fosterage** was an important means of
cementing alliances between groups. Nobles as well as commoners

placed their children at the age of seven in the homes of other families. A child and his foster parents often become exceptionally fond of each other, and it was foster parents who were called "Mother" and "Father." The bond that developed between foster brothers could endure for life.

The host family was paid for a foster child's upkeep. It cost more to place a girl—eight heifers and two cows—because girls required special protection. The sum for a boy was six heifers and one cow. While in her foster home, a commoner's daughter (if her family was well off enough to place her in one) learned to milk, make butter, cook, weave, and sew. A noble's daughter learned the art of fine embroidery, and to play a musical instrument, sing, and recite poetry. When they were fourteen, foster daughters returned to their birth families.

A commoner's son learned to farm or became skilled at a craft such as blacksmithing or woodworking. A nobleman's son learned the art of war, and to hunt, ride well, and play chess. He was older than his sister—seventeen—when he returned to his birth family. One result of fosterage was formal behavior between biological fathers and sons. Caesar observed that until a boy

The Changing Role of Women

After the Celts were Christianized, the position of women in their society changed dramatically. Divorce was prohibited, and women were required to submit to the will of their husbands. In A.D. 697, Adamnan's Law prohibited women from going to war, ending a Celtic custom that had lasted for centuries.

reached manhood, it was considered proper for him to stand but never sit in his father's presence.

Slavery Among the Celts

The ancient Celts had a deep love of personal freedom, yet denied freedom to others by keeping slaves. Chains and manacles found at La Tène and at Anglesey in Britain indicate that slaves were not only kept but also restrained. Pope Gregory I (c. A.D. 540–604) reported seeing child slaves for sale at markets in Britain. The Celts kept slaves for the same reason other cultures have: to do the "dirty" work they didn't want to do themselves. As importantly, slaves could be sold or traded, like livestock. The Celts didn't grow grapes from which to make wine, but since they were fond of drinking, slaves frequently were exchanged for Greek and Roman **amphorae** (clay containers) full of wine.

Many Celts kept slaves to do a variety of tasks. This metalwork shows a female slave serving a man, possibly her owner.

Food, Wine, and Feasts

Feasts were another important part of the lives of the Celts. Analysis of animal bones found at ancient Celtic sites indicates that although pork was considered the most favored meat, more than

Death: Better Than Slavery

Although the Celts enslaved others, they sometimes took their own lives rather than become slaves themselves. The result of Caesar's conquest of the Celts in Gaul in about 55 B.C. was that from a population of six to seven million Celts, a million were enslaved. After subduing the British Celts in the first century A.D., the Romans expected to be provided with—in addition to leather, corn, and grains—a steady supply of slaves.

50 percent of the meat consumed was beef. Wild game, such as deer and elk, was eaten as well. Fish, salmon in particular, was considered a delicacy. The Celts especially liked baked salmon seasoned with salt and vinegar.

One eyewitness account gives us a glimpse at the table manners of the Celts. Athenaeus, a Greek writer, watched Celts "raising up whole limbs [of roast beef] in both hands and biting off the meat." Pieces that were hard to tear off with their teeth were

Games and Pastimes

Celts were fond of board games and played one similar to chess called **fidchell**, or "wooden wisdom." A game played with dice, **branduh**, or "black raven," was unearthed by archaeologists at a site north of London in 1965. Images on clay engravings suggest a game similar to field hockey was played with a ball and stick, but the players competed while naked.

Stick-to-the-Ribs Recipe

Scottish Celts made a meal called **haggis**. The stomach of a slaughtered sheep was thoroughly washed and soaked overnight in water. "**Sheep's pluck**" (the animal's heart, lungs, and liver) was boiled for two hours. The meat was chopped, mixed with onions and salt, then packed into the clean stomach. The pouch was sewn shut, pricked to prevent bursting, put in a pot, and simmered for three hours. At serving time it was sliced open and spoonfuls of haggis were dished up.

cut with small daggers. The choicest serving of any meat was always presented to the bravest warrior at the gathering.

Large quantities of wine, beer, or mead were usually consumed at any Celtic feast. Diodorus Siculus said the Celts were "extremely partial to wine" and drank it unmixed. By contrast the Romans diluted their wine with water to avoid becoming too easily intoxicated. As often happens when strong alcohol is consumed, people become quarrelsome. Among the Celts a merry gathering could turn into a brawl marked by sword fights that led to a death. Such a murder would be avenged, beginning an endless cycle of revenge.

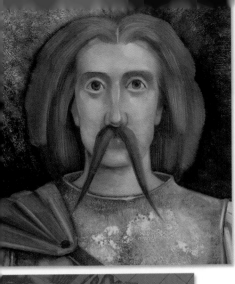

Chapter III

KINGS AND NOBLES

At the top of the Celtic social ladder were kings, who were thought to be almost divine. Each ***túath***, or tribe, large or small, followed its own king. Although kings of the smaller tribes didn't wield as much power as those with larger followings, their subjects were steadfastly loyal. Only a Druid (a Celtic priest) had more power than a king. When meetings were held to decide important matters, no king could speak until the priest did.

Kingship among the Celts was unique because a king's job wasn't to make laws or punish lawbreakers. He occupied himself with military matters: protecting his people against enemies, subduing weaker tribes, and acquiring more farmland on which to plant crops.

To become a king, a man was expected to be perfect in body and spirit. He must have no physical blemishes or handicaps. He must have proved his bravery in battle and be trustworthy. If a king became ill, he hoped for a speedy recovery or he'd be replaced. A kingship could be withdrawn if a king couldn't protect his people, if his health failed, if he produced no heirs, or if he simply got old. In extreme cases a king wasn't merely dethroned but might be executed for his imperfection.

Every member of the tribe financially supported his or her king. A king was owed yearly tribute—a tax—from all members of his tribe. It could be paid in land, livestock, crops, clothing, jewelry, weapons, slaves, even beer, wine, and mead. If a king had a large following and his warriors conquered new territories, he was able to accumulate considerable wealth.

Among the Irish Celts there were different types of kings. The **árd rí**, or high king, was the most divine king of all. When it was time to select such a king, a bull was slaughtered, and its meat was boiled. A Druid priest ate the meat, drank the sacred broth, then lay down to sleep on the bull's skin. As he drifted into sleep, chants were recited over him to help him dream of who should become the next high king. He was obliged to be truthful about his dream; if he deceived the tribe, he could be killed. Low kings owed tribute to the árd rí, as did other folk, and went to war on his behalf.

A Celtic king focused most of his efforts on the military. He was responsible for defending his people and conquering new lands.

When a king died, his sons, from oldest to youngest, were eligible to take his place. The dead king's other blood relatives—

Nuada of the Silver Hand

The health and success of a tribe was demonstrated by its leader. If a leader became ill or impaired, doubts were raised among his followers about their own well-being. A Celtic tale from Ireland told of King Nuada, who lost a hand in battle. The injury made him less than perfect, so he quickly had a new hand cast out of silver, complete with movable fingers and joints. Leaders of his tribe weren't convinced it was equal to a real hand and forced him to step aside for a man who was more fit.

brothers, nephews, and grandsons—also were eligible. With many candidates to choose from, family feuds often developed, and if not resolved peacefully resulted in revenge and bloodshed. Occasionally kingship was determined by combat, as branches of a family or tribe faced off against each other. Among the Irish Celts a would-be king didn't fight the battle himself but was represented by an **airechta**, a man who championed his cause.

Not All Celtic Rulers Were Men

Boudicca and Cartimandua, real-life queens of the British Celts, commanded tribes and led warriors into battle. According to myth, after the death of her father, Macha Mong Ruad, "Macha of the Red Hair," daughter of Aod Ruad, the high king of Ireland, killed a man who tried to prevent her from becoming queen. Ireland's ancient capital, Emhain Macha, or "Twins of Macha" (in modern Ulster Province), was said to have been named in honor of her twin sons.

This statue is believed to be of a Celtic prince. It was discovered near Glauburg, Germany.

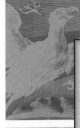

Five Sons, One Throne

Eochaid Muighmedon, árd rí of Ireland in about A.D. 350, had five sons. To discover which of the five made the wisest decisions, the king ordered the royal smithy, or blacksmith workshop, to be set on fire. Brian rescued the chariots; Ailill saved the swords and shields; Fiacrha dragged away the water trough; the most foolish son packed off firewood. Only Niall possessed the common sense to carry the blacksmith's anvil and tools to safety—and became high king upon his father's death.

Royal Burial for a Mighty Leader

In 1978, an archaeological team led by Jorg Biel excavated an Iron Age burial mound at Hochdorf, Germany. The 50-ton roof covering the 30-foot (9.1-m) deep chamber had collapsed, reducing the height of the crypt to 5 feet (1.5 m). The interior had remained waterproof for 2,500 years, while oxidation (rust) from copper and bronze vessels delayed the decomposition of many once-living items.

Buried beneath debris, the skeletal remains of a Celtic warrior-king were found on a 9-foot (3-m) bronze couch. Examination of the bones indicated the man was forty to fifty years of age and about 6 feet (2 m) tall. He'd rested through the centuries on a mattress of hemp fibers covered with animal furs, wore a gold **torque** around his neck and a gold belt around his waist. Nearby were remnants of flowers, suggesting the burial took place in summer. A vessel that once had held mead and bronze and iron drinking horns were close at hand.

Sacred Wedding at Tara

A high king married a mortal woman and hoped to sire many sons, but his true bride was not human. His real bride was the land itself. The land provided everything a tribe needed to live: water to drink, fertile fields to plant, animals to eat.

Among the Celts of Ireland, a king was symbolically married to the land in a ceremony at **Tara**, the center of their kingdom in modern-day County Meath. At Tara a goddess dwelled in ***Lia Fail***, the Stone of Destiny, a large, upright rock rising out of the surrounding plain. The goddess—sometimes represented by a white

According to lore, the stone of destiny stood on this burial mound.

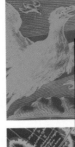

Comforts of a King's Court

If you were the guest of a Celtic king you could count on being well treated. After you returned from a day of hunting deer, a bath scented with oils and herbs awaited you. At dinner you enjoyed platters of roast venison, beef, pork, and fowl. Bowls were filled with fresh fruits, vegetables, and nuts; drinking horns were filled (often!) with mead or wine. Musicians, dancers, and jugglers entertained you. Bards finished the evening with songs and stories celebrating the courage of your host.

mare—called out her approval if she agreed with the choice that was made. When a king had been chosen, he and his nobles attended **Feis Temhra**, the Feast of Tara, symbolizing his marriage to the earth.

Arthur: The Mythical Celtic King

Evidence for a "real" King Arthur is scanty. Scholars agree the man we call King Arthur probably is a combination of several mythic figures. The name Artorius comes from the Latin word *ursus*, which is derived from the Greek word for "bear," *arktos*. A Celtic name, **Arddu** (pronounced AR-thyew), "the dark one," might have been the origin of Arthur's name. Tales about a Celtic chieftain named Arthur became so popular that Henry II claimed to be Arthur's true-life descendant when he came to the British throne in 1154.

In about A.D. 810, Arthur's name appeared in print for the first time in the *Historia Brittonum*. In 1136, an Oxford scholar devoted fifty pages of *History of the Kings of Britain* to an account of Arthur's life. In 1180, in *Perceval, or The Story of the Grail* by Chrétien de Troyes, a French poet, Arthur's court was identified as Camelot, a fortified city at Tintagel in southern England. Sir Thomas Malory wrote *Le Morte d'Arthur*, "The Death of Arthur," in 1470, and introduced other elements to the Arthurian legend: Merlin the magician, the Lady of the Lake, and Guinevere, as well as the Sword in the Stone.

The Legend of King Arthur

Arthur began life as the son of Uther Pendragon, king of all Britain. The king died when Arthur was two years old, and the boy was raised as the foster son of Sir Ector. When the kingdom fell into chaos, Merlin invited worthy men to London, where feasts, games, and tournaments were held to decide who would be the next ruler of Britain. As noblemen arrived, they passed a churchyard where a stone supported a steel anvil holding a sword. A message on the anvil read *Whoso pulleth oute this swerd of this stone and anvyld [anvil] is rightwys kynge borne of all Brytaygne.*

Almost as Famous

Merlin was one of the most mysterious men in Western literature. He was a bearded, godlike figure whose Welsh name was Myrddin. He probably is a combination of several pagan figures going back to the Celtic Druids, for among his powers was the ability to foretell the future.

King Arthur is said to be a mythical figure, possibly formed from the stories of several men.

Sir Ector attended the celebration with twelve-year-old Arthur. Many tried to pull the sword from the stone, but only Arthur was successful, and so began his long reign as the king of Britain. With many brave knights at his side, Arthur conquered monsters, defended the downtrodden, and fought for justice. But the most enduring symbol of King Arthur's reign was the

The Chalice of the Cross

In ancient mythology, a magic vessel provided a never-ending supply of food for those who needed it. The legend was refashioned by Christian monks to reflect Christian beliefs. It was called "the chalice of the Cross," a vessel used by Jesus and his disciples at the Last Supper. Joseph was said to have used it to catch blood that flowed from his son's wounds at the Crucifixion. After Jesus's death Joseph took the vessel and fled to Britain, where he founded an abbey at Glastonbury. Before his death he secretly buried the Grail, and men have searched for it ever since.

search for the Holy Grail. Various legends have described the Grail as a chalice that held sacred wine, a large bowl, or simply a blinding white light.

When King Arthur died, three queens, including his half-sister Morgan Le Fay, carried his body to a ship that sailed to Avalon, far beyond the western horizon, among the Isles of the Blessed. "Yet some men say that King Arthur is not dead," wrote Malory. A stone beneath the water near Avalon is said to bear an inscription:

Hic Lacet Arthurus Rex Quondam Rexque Futurus

Here Lies Arthur, the Once and Future King

According to legend Arthur and his knights will rise from their watery graves to serve Britain again in its hour of need.

Chapter IV

DRUIDS, GODS, AND WITCHES

To the Celts, the natural and supernatural worlds were insepa-rable. Lakes, rivers, bogs, rocks, trees, and hills were sacred because they were places humankind and spirits could enter each other's kingdoms. Human beings had to be careful at such sites, for they might stumble into the spirit world and be unable to leave. It wasn't necessarily a horrible fate. In **Tir na n-Og**, the "Land of Youth," no one ever grew old. Magic apple trees were always loaded with fruit; a pig slaughtered for a feast one day came back to life the next; wine jugs were never empty.

The spirits communicated with human beings through signs and symbols that could be difficult for ordinary mortals to understand. What did it mean when clouds in the sky took a certain shape, when waves on the sea whitened with foam, when the wind suddenly changed direction? Various ani-mals—deer, horses, and boars; rabbits, mice, and squirrels; even birds such as ravens, swans, and cormorants—might be

Differing Opinions of the Druids

Scholars and rulers of the ancient world were divided in their opinions of the Druids. Caesar dismissed their beliefs as superstition. Strabo regarded the Druids with respect and revulsion—respect for their learning, revulsion at their practice of human sacrifice. After the Celts were conquered by the Romans, Emperor Tiberius banned the Druids, believing they were evil, not holy. However, **fir fer**, or "fair play," a principle of Druidic law, prompted some scholars, such as Clement of Alexandria and Hippolytus of Greece, to call Druids ***magistri sapientica***, or "masters of wisdom," equal to the great philosophers of Egypt, Persia, and India.

spirits in disguise. Kings and commoners alike needed guidance, and it was Druids who provided it.

Pliny the Elder, a Roman naturalist of the first century A.D., said the name the Celts gave their priests—Druids—came from the Indo-European word **dru**, or oak. One of the holiest places in Druid lore was **Drunemeton**, or "oak sanctuary," which may have been in Asia or Gaul (present-day France). Men (and some women) became Druids after they learned "the knowledge of the oak."

Sacred Ceremonies

Groves of oak trees were so sacred to the Druids that ordinary persons were forbidden to enter them on penalty of death. Between dusk and dawn, when the spirits were most active, even Druids themselves took care. Common folk dreaded oak

An illustration depicts the sacred grove of the Druids.

groves so much they walked miles out of their way to avoid passing through one.

Oaks were revered not merely as trees but for what grew on their branches. "Druids hold nothing more sacred than mistletoe," Pliny wrote. Mistletoe, a parasitic plant with small yellow-green leaves and white berries, grows on oak branches. Mistletoe was used in Druidic religious ceremonies, and could be harvested only by priests, only at certain times.

Education of Druid Priests

The Celts had an oral tradition. They didn't read or write. Without books to consult, everything Druid students needed to learn was passed orally from teacher to student and memorized. They were instructed on the history of Celtic tribes, stories of the gods, laws of astronomy and medicine, rules followed by judges in court, and how to mediate between the worlds of men and spirits.

It took up to twenty years for students to commit to memory everything they needed to know. Once

Some of the Druids conducted human sacrifices. They believed that these sacrifices would please their gods.

Druid apprentices completed their education and were able to speak "the language of the gods," they became not only priests but teachers, healers, judges, philosophers, and magicians.

Secrets and Sacrifices

The Druids kept many secrets from their own people. After the Roman conquests in Gaul and Britain, they also hid their activities from the Romans. Secrecy increased rather decreased the Druids' power, for if no one was sure what they did, it was easy to imagine that they could do anything. Druids were said to cast spells that brought a rain of blood and fire across the land. They erected invisible "Druid fences" on battlefields to protect Celtic warriors from harm. Priests received messages from the stars that had been transmitted by the gods.

The Romans criticized the Celts for sacrificing human beings. The Celts' sacrifice of men and women wasn't for entertainment, however. It was connected to certain religious rituals and was a way to appease the gods or foretell the future. The discovery of

Harvesting Mistletoe

On the sixth night of the moon's journey, when it was shaped like a crescent, two white bulls were led to an oak grove. A white-robed Druid climbed a tree and cut mistletoe with a gold knife, also shaped like a crescent. Afterward, the bulls were sacrificed and eaten.

Mistletoe, boiled and given in a drink, was said to cure infertility in humans and animals and was an antidote (remedy) for poisoning. Modern science suggests mistletoe might aid in the treatment of high blood pressure and certain tumors.

Trances and Visions

Evidence of the use of **cannabis** (marijuana, a member of the nettle family) was found in graves at Hallstatt. Scholars believe the Druids probably used this drug to induce trances or visions that helped them interpret messages that had been sent from the spirit world.

well-preserved bodies in Denmark and Britain indicates some type of ritual killing had been carried out, whose significance scholars don't yet understand.

Celtic Spirits and Divinities

The worship of particular gods and goddesses varied somewhat throughout the Celtic world. Pictures on tablets celebrating Taranis, the Celtic god of storms and thunder, have been found in such diverse places as Britain, France, Germany, and the former Yugoslavia. Taranis demanded human sacrifices and also was associated with the sacred eight-spoked wheel of the year. The home of Sequana, goddess of healing, was located near Dijon, France. Sulis presided at Bath, England. The images of the gods of war, Cocidius and Belatucadrus, could be found near Hadrian's Wall in northern Britain. Many ancient religions originated with worship of a mother goddess; among the Celts she was called Danu, for whom the Danube River is named.

Bridget, the goddess of the hearth, ruled over medicine. Boann, "mother of the herds," was associated with white cows; the river Boyne, west of Dublin, was named in her honor. The goddess Epona was the protector of horses; Artio represented

Druid Universities

Two large centers were among several places where Druid priests were educated in ancient times. One was located west of the modern-day city of Paris, the other on the island of Anglesey along the coast of Wales. Caesar said the purpose of such education was to prepare priests to "officiate at the worship of the gods, regulate public and private sacrifices, give rulings on all religious questions . . . and act as judges in practically all disputes whether between tribes or between individuals."

Taranis (center) was the god of storms and thunder.

bears; Arduinna was the defender of boars. Among male gods, Dagda, the Good God, was master of life and death as well as the bringer of prosperity and abundance. Lugh of the Long Hand, the god of war, took as his familiars (animals that shared his power) the cock, turtle, and goat.

Women had a role in the Celtic religion. They served as Druidesses.

Women Priests and Witches

Women as well as men became priests. Romans themselves sometimes were advised by flesh-and-blood Druidesses. As the third-century Roman emperor Severus Alexander was about to go into battle, a Druidess warned, "Do not hope for victory, and put no trust in your soldiers." The emperor shrugged off her words. He was defeated in battle, then murdered by his own men.

Warrior-goddesses such as Morrígan, Medh, Macha, and Badb also possessed **himbas forosnai**, or foresight, and could foretell the fate of warriors on the battlefield. Fedelma, who came from the Otherworld, was a poet as well. She was easily recognized because she always wore a speckled cloak, and her eyes had no pupils. Fedelma warned the Celts of doom on a battlefield by crying out, "I see it crimson, I see it red!"

Warriors who had been taken captive were also used by Druidesses to predict the outcome of battle. Strabo described the execution of prisoners during times of war.

Magic Spindles

The bodies of several elderly women, dating from the third and fourth century A.D., were found at Winchester and Dorset in Britain. The bodies were accompanied by spindles, slender wood rods on which thread or yarn was wound as it was spun. According to Celtic myth, spindles were associated with fate; a witch could end someone's life simply by snapping the thread she was winding on her spindle.

Gray-haired Druid priestesses dressed in white gowns advanced upon a prisoner. One of them "crowned" the victim by lightly touching the tip of her sword to his head. The man was killed, his blood collected in a sacred bronze vessel. After death his body was opened, and the entrails (intestines) studied for signs of Celtic victory or defeat in the battle taking place.

Witches were ranked below the Druid priestesses and were feared more than revered. They represented the darker aspects of the supernatural world and often appeared in threes. Stories from the *Mabinogion*, a collection of tales from ancient Wales, tell of the Nine Witches of Gloucester—three groups of three—that were destroyed by the Welsh hero Peredur and King Arthur.

After the Romans conquered the people of Gaul, efforts were made to get rid of all Druids, but throughout world history, attempts to stamp out religious beliefs have been difficult. The Druids continued their practices in greater secrecy than before, and their beliefs prevail in various forms into modern times.

Chapter V

ARTISANS AND STORYTELLERS

Ancient Greek and Roman writers often described the Celts as barbarians who loved to fight and drank too much wine. The discovery of Celtic arts and crafts at Hallstatt and La Tène among many other sites, demonstrated that the People of Iron appreciated beauty as keenly as did the elite of the Mediterranean. When Celtic literature was rediscovered in the Middle Ages, it was further evidence that Celtic culture was sophisticated as well as savage.

Celtic Jewelry

The Celts, especially members of the noble class, put high value on personal adornment. A remarkable piece of sixth-century jewelry unearthed at Hallstatt demonstrates that the Celts enjoyed art that had two purposes—to please the eye and the ear. A bronze brooch, decorated with tiny circles representing the sun, supports twelve triangles dangling from delicate chains. When the wearer moved or danced, the triangles created the sound similar to that created by wind chimes.

The Celts adorned their arms, wrists, fingers, and ankles with jewelry made of gold, silver, and bronze. Large gold disks dating from about 800 to 600 B.C. were used as hair ornaments.

Torques, or neck rings made of braided strands of gold, were often hinged in the middle so they could be easily placed around a wearer's neck. In place of buttons, beautifully designed fasteners of gold, silver, or bronze held garments together.

The Celts made necklaces of **amber** (hard, fossilized tree resin that can be cut and polished), and during the third century B.C., glass bracelets became fashionable. Metal oxides were added during the glassmaking process to produce specific colors: cobalt yielded blue (the Celts' favorite color), copper made green, lead made yellow, iron made red. Sometimes pieces of colored glass were inlaid on metal jewelry and on horse ornaments.

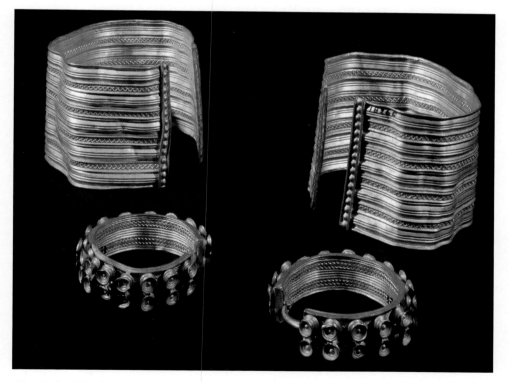

The Celts liked to decorate themselves with beautiful jewelry, such as these gold earrings and bracelets.

Exciting Discoveries

A first-century B.C. cauldron was discovered in pieces in 1891 by peat cutters working in a bog near Gundestrup, Denmark and has been the subject of much debate. The bowl, which analysis proved was 97 percent pure silver, was made in sections, measured 27 inches (68.6 centimeters) in diameter when assembled, and weighed almost 20 pounds (9 kilograms). The pieces were cleaned, reassembled, and the vessel now is displayed at the National Museum of Denmark in Copenhagen.

There are more than one hundred images on the Gundestrup Cauldron depicting many different types of figures, such as hunting hounds, panthers, bulls, serpents, griffins, soldiers, and men blowing war trumpets. Centered at the bottom inside the vessel is an image of a dying bull. While many of these images are considered to be Celtic motifs, or ideas and symbols that appear in a piece of art or literature, scholars think it may have been made by another culture. There has been much debate about whether the cauldron is truly a Celtic object.

Another fascinating discovery of the handiwork of Celtic artisans was made in 1953 when archaeologists unearthed a

Celtic Cosmetics

Celtic women painted their fingernails and reddened their cheeks with dye made from **ruan**, an herb. They darkened their brows with berry juice, and wealthy women were able to admire the results in beautifully decorated mirrors. In 1908, a mirror used by a Celt in the first century B.C. was found at Desborough, England, when a site was excavated to build a factory.

While the Gundestrup Cauldron features some Celtic symbolism, it is still being debated by scholars whether it was made by the Celts.

2,500-year-old tomb at Vix in central France. The skeleton of a Celtic woman lay on a wooden cart inside the tomb. Although her exact rank can't be determined, she was named the "Princess of Vix." Examination of the princess's bones revealed she was about thirty-five years old and had been laid to rest with care. As befits royalty her shroud was made of leather, not ordinary linen. She wore a gold torque and other jewelry. A 66-inch (167.6-cm), 350-pound (157.7-kg) Greek **krater**, or bronze wine vessel, was found in the tomb, indicating that her tribe traded with the people of the Mediterranean.

Celtic Weavers

Weavers supplied the Celts with the colorful cloth they loved. Celtic women, skilled weavers of linen and wool, created fabrics

The Color of Kings

Purple dye was so costly in ancient times that purple was called "the color of kings" because only kings or nobles could afford it. After some investigation it was discovered that the color came from the **murex** shellfish, which possesses a gland that oozes a fluid that turns purple when exposed to sunlight. It requires 1,200 shellfish to produce 1.6 grams of dye, making it equal in value to gold.

patterned with stripes, checks, and plaids. They made dyes from plants to achieve the colors they liked best, such as blue, red, yellow, green, black, and occasionally purple. Garments often were decorated with fine embroidery, the edges of shawls finished with long fringes or tiny bells. Garments of the nobility often had gold thread woven into the fabric, and collars and cuffs were trimmed with fox or wolf fur.

Animals in Celtic Art

The outline of a white horse 350 feet (106.7 m) long was carved into the chalk hills of Uffington in Oxfordshire, England, in roughly 1000 B.C. and is plainly visible today. It likely was a tribute to a horse god, for white horses were sacred among the Celts. Birds, especially crows and ravens, were frequently depicted in Celtic artwork and stories; they were associated with death because they were black and fed on the flesh of the dead.

Wild boars, admired for their aggressive behavior, often appeared in Celtic art. A favorite way to portray the boar was as the animal was about to charge, bristles raised along its spine.

This aerial photograph provides an excellent view of the white horse carving in Uffington, England.

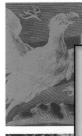

Wheels of Iron

Carts and war chariots had their wooden wheels rimmed with iron, which made them more durable than plain wood. Celtic blacksmiths shaped iron rims slightly smaller than the wooden wheels of the carts or chariots they were meant to fit. When the rim was reheated, it expanded slightly and was forced over the edge of the wheel. The metal shrank as it cooled, creating a tight fit.

Although the Celts ate mostly beef, the meat of boars was preferred for important feasts.

Amazing Metalworkers

In Iron Age culture no craftsperson was more important than the blacksmith. He made weapons for war—swords, daggers, and horse gear, but also for peace—plows, scythes, and sickles. From early times Celts regarded metalworkers as having magical powers, for they turned common earth—ore containing iron, silver, or gold—into works of usefulness and beauty. Metalsmiths of the La Tène culture decorated sword scabbards and belt hooks with elaborate scrollwork and figures of animals, birds, and humans. The Celts' interest in wine drinking is evident from the many metal drinking cups that have been recovered at burial sites.

Metalsmiths also made the currency used by the Celts. They began making coins in about the third century B.C., probably as the result of having seen Greek coins. Silver coins were used in the region of the Danube River; gold was preferred in the area from Bohemia to Britain. Coins, fifty at a time, were made by placing disks of melted gold or silver in a press. The lid of the press was

The Celts valued blacksmiths for their incredible skills. They were able to make strong, sturdy, and beautiful objects, such as this helmet.

closed, then struck with a hammer. A design was imprinted on each side of the warm metal. The small size of some coins—0.35 inch (9 millimeters) in diameter—indicated the level of the Celtic coin makers' skill.

Poets and Storytellers

Two kinds of storytellers shared the task of transmitting Celtic culture from generation to generation: Druids and bards (also called *filidh*). Druid priests ministered to religious and political needs; the bards' main task was to celebrate the brave deeds of kings, nobles, and warriors. Bards weren't men who simply told stories for entertainment, though. Like Druid priests, they belonged to a skilled elite whose education took many years.

Bards were attached to the household of a patron but were free to travel about, publicizing the deeds of the person they served. Bards also created chants to celebrate births, deaths, and weddings, and issued prophecies. Among the Irish Celts as a bard slept, he hoped to dream about the *leanon sidh*, the "learning fairy," who might give him special knowledge. Certain bards had the power to chase away ghosts and evil spirits. On a more practical level they also rid homes and villages of rats and illness.

A Celtic Tale: The Children of Lir

The tale of the Children of Lir illustrates the Celts' fascination with the destructive power of jealousy. After Lir's wife died, his friends feared he'd never recover from grief. "No man should live

Music and Dancing

Ancient writers said little about Celtic music other than its use in war. A stone figure found in Brittany dating to about 70 B.C. indicates the Celts were entertained by harpists in more peaceful settings. A bronze figure found at Neuvy-en-Sullias in France as well as images on pottery indicate that dancing was performed on ceremonial occasions. The Gundestrup cauldron also depicts dancing figures.

THE BARD.

W. Theed, Sculp.r 1858.

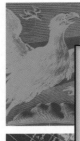

Images of Celebration

In 1861, many small bronze statues varying in size from 4 to 9 inches (10 to 23 cm) in height were discovered by French quarry workers near the city of Orléans. Hidden for almost 2,000 years, the images of musicians, priests, jugglers, and dancers are thought to reflect the way the Celts celebrated festivals. Archaeologists believe the statues were buried hastily to hide them from invading Romans.

unwed," said Bodb the Red. "My daughters, three of the loveliest maidens in the kingdom, live in my court. I invite you to pick one for a wife."

Lir chose Aeb, the eldest. The pair began a new life in Lir's castle atop the Hill of the White Field. Two sets of twins were born, but alas, Aeb died. Lir's four beautiful children were his only comfort. Bodb the Red again offered a daughter in marriage. Lir picked Aoife, who seemed pleased to become a stepmother for her sister's children. But soon she grew jealous of the love Lir showed children and decided to slay them.

Aoife set out with her stepchildren, and along the way she ordered the servants to kill them. "It is a dreadful deed you ask," they said, and refused to obey. Aoife seized a sword to murder them herself, but she too was unable to commit such a crime. By evening the carriage arrived at the edge of Loch Dairbhreach. Aoife invited the children to refresh themselves in the lake. As they entered the water, she touched each with a magic wand and one by one they turned into white swans as she chanted:

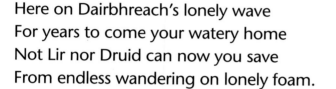

Shakespeare's Inspiration

Centuries later William Shakespeare of London's Globe Theatre heard the tale of Lir and his children. He was inspired to write *King Lear*, a play first performed in 1606, translated into many languages, and still performed on stages around the world—a Celtic tale of jealousy that endures.

Here on Dairbhreach's lonely wave
For years to come your watery home
Not Lir nor Druid can now you save
From endless wandering on lonely foam.

Lir hurried to the lake when he learned of his children's fate and was greeted by the four beautiful swans. "Do not mourn," they said. "Your love will give us strength to endure a thousand years."

Three hundred years passed, followed by three hundred years, then by three hundred more. At the end of a thousand years, the swans died. Their snowy feathers fell away to reveal ancient human creatures. They were buried by villagers beneath a stone inscribed, "Here lie the children of Lir, who rest in peace at last."

Chapter VI

WARRIORS AND WARRIOR QUEENS

"The whole race [is] . . . madly fond of war, high-spirited and quick to battle," Strabo wrote of the Celts. Livy had a different opinion: "Always they bring more smoke than fire." Both descriptions contained some truth.

Other reports shed light on the Celts' philosophy and its impact on their warriors. After the Romans recovered from the shock of their first battlefield encounters with the Celts, they discovered that sound military strategy could turn the tables on the barbarians. Even so, the Celts possessed one trait that made them a dreaded foe. They weren't afraid to die. Their indifference was based on the religious belief that in the afterlife, life would continue on as it did on Earth, except there would be no hunger, no sickness, and no aging. It was a conviction that made them heedless even in the face of certain death.

Weapons of War

A scabbard made of iron, bronze, or leather held a broad sword that hung from a warrior's belt. It was decorated with elaborate images of animals, birds, or mythical creatures. A warrior also carried a short, broad knife for close fighting and a spear that could be thrown as a javelin.

Sling stones were hurled from a leather loop that was swung round overhead and then released. An arsenal of 20,000 sling stones was found in a pit inside the eastern gate of Maiden Castle

More Reckless Than Ever

The drama of a battle often seemed more important to the Celts than its outcome. Livy reported that the Celts grew bored after they laid siege to Rome in 391 B.C. They wandered off to "lie at night like animals on the bank of some stream—unprotected, unguarded, no watches set . . . more reckless than ever." Cú Chulainn, a mythic Celtic warrior, summed up the Celts' attitude: If he could be remembered for courage in battle it didn't matter "if I am but one day and one night in this world."

The Celts were known for being fierce warriors.

in Dorset, England. No archaeological evidence has been discovered indicating that the ancient Celts used bows or arrows, nor did words for "bow" or "arrow" appear in the early Celtic language.

Music was another weapon used in battle. The terror created by the Celts as they filled "the air with hideous songs . . . and the dreadful noise as they beat their shields" sometimes made an all-out assault on an enemy unnecessary, according to Livy. Carnyxes, bronze or wooden trumpets as tall as a man with bells shaped like the heads of wild animals, created a harsh sound that suited the chaos of battle.

For protection warriors carried shields. Celtic shields were rectangular in shape and large enough to protect a warrior from neck to knee. The shields usually were made of wood, leather, or a combination of both, and covered with leather. The edges were bound with leather strips, the handhold protected by an **umbo**, a padded leather cover for a warrior's fist. In spite of their size the shields were light and flexible. Shields of this type, dating from the first century A.D., can be seen today on a Roman-built archway at Orange in southern France.

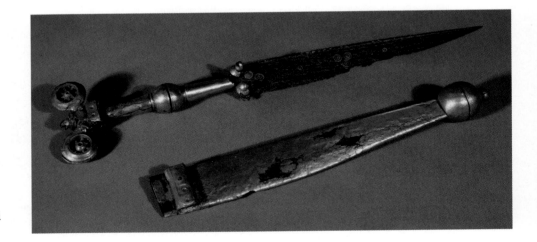

A dagger, such as the one shown, would have been used for fighting an enemy close up.

Code of Honor

Celtic warriors lived by a code of honor that was simple but is still timely.

- Treat women and children kindly.
- Do not boast or be stubborn.
- Bear no tales and tell no lies.
- Do not drink too much in taverns.
- Be ready to give rather than take.

Dressed for War

Warriors of all cultures wear armor to protect their bodies—helmets, breastplates, coverings for arms and legs—as well as uniforms to distinguish themselves from an enemy. Celtic helmets were made of bronze or iron. Projections in the shape of bulls' or rams' horns, or winged birds made a warrior's head look impressively large. Considering the Celts' height, such helmets must have increased their fearsome appearance.

However, Greek and Roman soldiers were shocked to witness the Celts going into battle stark naked. They wore nothing save sword belts, gold torques (neck rings), and gold

Some Celts had elaborate helmets, such as this one featuring two large horns. It is thought that the horns may be a symbol of the gods. This helmet was found in the Thames River in England.

bands around their upper arms. The writer Polybius believed the Celts removed their clothing to improve their freedom of movement. Modern scholars have concluded that nakedness had an important religious significance.

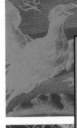

A Barbaric Practice

Roman troops themselves were merciless warriors, but they were revolted by the Celtic practice of beheading enemies. The Celts hung their victims' heads from the necks of their horses or above the doors of their houses. The Celts didn't consider the practice as barbaric, but as a way to honor a brave foe. Such trophies also were dried, preserved with cedar oil, and proudly displayed to visitors.

Found at La Tène, this doorway is decorated with the skulls of enemies.

On certain ritual occasions, the Celts painted their naked bodies with blue dye made from leaves of the **woad** plant. Added to their fierce cries, naked, blue-bodied warriors must have struck horror in the hearts of an enemy. In 1987, a well-preserved human body dating from about A.D. 50–100 was discovered in a peat bog in Britain. Traces of blue dye could still be seen on the man's skin.

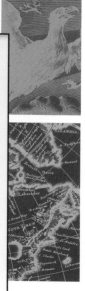

Golden Torques

In 391 B.C., a Roman soldier killed a Celtic chieftain who fought naked except for a shield, sword, and gold torque. Forever after he was called "Torquatus." When Roman troops overran the Celts at Bologna, Italy, in 191 B.C., they took 1,500 gold torques from the battlefield. In 1948, when a farm field in Norfolk, England, was plowed, a large collection of torques was unearthed. A gold torque found in Germany measured 12 inches (30 cm) in circumference and weighed more than 13 pounds (4.8 kg).

War Chariots

A Celtic war chariot was a lightweight, wooden cart built for speed and quick handling. It consisted of a wooden platform connected by a wood pole and yoke to a pair of horses. (The horses were so small we'd call them ponies today.) The sides of the chariot were made of wicker—slender, bendable tree branches—with the front and back left open to allow a warrior to jump on or off.

Celtic chariots carried two men: a driver and warrior. The driver often was a freeman chosen from the poorer classes. Sometimes the chariot driver was the warrior's wife or sister. These chariots careened along at a breakneck pace, their iron-rimmed wheels adding a clatter to the din of trumpets, snorting horses, and warriors' shouts.

Julius Caesar saw such carts firsthand during his invasion of Britain in 54 B.C. He faced Cassivellaunus, commander of 4,000 charioteers with "the mobility of cavalry and the staying power of infantry," Caesar wrote. The Celts trained daily until they were so "expert that they can control their horses at full gallop . . . and turn them in a moment."

The Celts' First Warrior-King

In 52 B.C., Caesar brought the might of the Roman army to bear on the Celtic tribes in Gaul. When important matters in Rome caused him to leave the field, the Celts saw a chance for victory. They joined together and rose up against Roman domination, a rebellion Caesar blamed on "meetings at secluded spots in the woods" conducted by the Druids.

The Celts had never united under a single warlord, but now they named Vercingetorix, a prince of the Arverni tribe, as their commander. When he assumed leadership of other tribes, including the Senones, Parisii, Cadurci, and Turoni, Vercingetorix became the first Celt ever to wield such power.

It was winter, and Vercingetorix believed the snow-covered mountains would make Caesar's swift return to Gaul unlikely. But

Warriors for Hire

Celtic recruits sometimes became professional mercenaries, or warriors for hire. They willingly switched allegiance from one chieftain to another, depending on who offered the best pay. Nor did such warriors serve only the Celts. In 218 B.C., when the Carthaginian general Hannibal marched across the Alps, Celtic mercenaries joined him. Later, they found themselves fighting against their own kin.

Caesar knew he must take strong action if he wanted to subdue the unruly tribes permanently. He ordered his soldiers to shovel a path through 6-foot (2-m) snowdrifts and took the Celts by surprise.

A Most Ingenious People

The Celts, famous for their wild frenzy in battle, changed their tactics under Vercingetorix's leadership. They "resorted to all kinds of devices; for they are a most ingenious people, and very clever at borrrowing and applying ideas," Caesar wrote. He praised Vercingetorix as a man of "boundless energy," yet the Celts were no match for the Romans. The king of the Lemovices

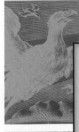

Taste for Conflict

Celtic women were much like their fathers, brothers, and husbands when it came to conflict. They were considered to be "high-spirited," in Strabo's words.

Pottery containers unearthed from graves in Hungary, dating from 700 B.C., depict women fighting and pulling each other's hair.

tribe was killed. Vercingetorix's cousin Vercassivellaunos was captured. Famine became widespread. Vercingetorix encouraged his followers to kill him and carry his head to the Romans as a symbol of defeat. They declined, so he surrendered.

Caesar forced the defeated Celts to accept Roman rule. Some who wouldn't fled to Britain. More than one million Celts were slain, another million enslaved. In 46 B.C., after playing a cat-and-mouse game with Vercingetorix for six years, Caesar paraded him through the streets of Rome, then executed him.

Warrior Queens

In peacetime Celtic women enjoyed many privileges. In wartime they went into battle, laying down their lives as willingly as men did. Tacitus reported military raids in A.D. 71 and A.D. 83 that were led by female commanders whose armies contained more women than men.

One of the best known warrior queens was Boudicca. Boudicca's name came from the Celtic word *bouda*, or "victory." When her husband, king of the Iceni tribe, died in Britain in about A.D. 60, Boudicca assumed the throne, her right by Celtic law. The Romans, who invaded Britain after their defeat of the Gauls, ignored the custom. They seized Boudicca, scourged (flogged) her in public, and attacked her daughters.

Boudicca urged the Iceni to rebel against Roman rule and made her own reasons clear. "I am descended from mighty men," she said in a speech recorded by Tacitus. "But I am not fighting for my kingdom and my wealth. I am fighting as an ordinary person for my lost freedom, my bruised body, and my outraged daughters."

The Iceni and other Celtic tribes rallied to Boudicca's call. Under her command they sacked Camulodunum (modern Colchester) along the Colne River. The Roman Ninth Infantry, sent to defend the settlement, was massacred. Boudicca marched toward Londinium (modern London), slaying all who opposed her, taking special revenge on Roman women.

Boudicca practiced war the way her Celtic ancestors had. She and her warriors were followed by supply wagons and entire families of women, children, and old people. On the plains of the British Midlands, it was a recipe for defeat. Tacitus calculated that 80,000 Celts were killed; the Romans lost 400. Boudicca and her daughters poisoned themselves rather than be captured. In 1902, eighteen centuries after their death, a statue of the warrior queen and her daughters was erected on the bank of the Thames River.

A sculpture from the early second century B.C. shows a Celtic woman in battle.

Cartimandua, Queen of the Brigantes

Unlike Boudicca, who became queen after the death of her husband, Cartimandua was queen of the Brigantes in her own right. She ruled the largest Celtic domain in Britain, including modern-day Cheshire, North and South Yorkshire, and Lancashire. Although the Romans had subdued most of the southern Celtic tribes, the Brigantes, Ordovices, and Silures maintained their

No Ordinary Queen

Boudicca was "tall, terrible to look on and gifted with a powerful voice," Cassius Dio reported. "A flood of bright red hair ran down to her knees," and the wheels of her war chariot were said to be fitted with knives that slashed enemies who came too near. She aroused "dread in all who set eyes upon her."

independence. When King Caradoc urged the Celts to join forces against the Romans, Cartimandua pretended to agree, but secretly allied herself with the Romans.

After King Caradoc's family was captured, he fled to the safest place he could think of: Cartimandua's estate. She put him in chains and handed him to the enemy. The enraged Brigantes turned against her and drove her into exile. While Boudicca was honored in song, story, and sculpture, Celtic mothers used stories of Cartimandua's fate to warn their daughters about the perils of betrayal.

Chapter VII

THE CELTS' LAST KINGDOM

Even before Caesar triumphed over the Celtic tribes in Gaul, he decided he must punish the British because they'd come to the aid of their kin during the Roman campaigns. Although Caesar once said Britain was a place where "all created things come to an end," he organized an invasion of the island that lay beyond what today is called the English Channel.

Caesar might well have wanted to punish the British Celts, but other reasons affected his decision. The conquest of Britain would give Rome access to Celtic goods, such as gold, silver, tin, timber, cattle, and slaves. Tribute extracted from Britain would help pay off the war debt incurred by fighting in Gaul. Control of the island would prevent the increasingly powerful Germanic tribes from gaining a foothold in Britain.

Setting the Stage for Battle

Caesar launched an invasion of Britain in 55 B.C. His fleet landed and his troops engaged in battle, but were unsuccessful. A second invasion commenced a year later, in July of 54 B.C. The weather held as 30,000 soldiers, including 2,000 cavalry, were loaded into 800 vessels for the crossing. Caesar was surprised by the fierce resistance he faced, for he was met

A later illustration imagines a meeting between Celtic war-leader Cassivellaunus and Caesar.

head-on by thousands of Celtic warriors under the leadership of war-leader Cassivellaunus. "The enemy never fought in close order, but in small parties," Caesar complained. Even so, the Celts were defeated by the Romans' superior military experience.

Under Roman Rule

Celtic kings, whether they lived in Gaul or in Britain, often mistrusted each other. After the Roman invasion the presence of foreigners among them further undermined their relationships. Rather than unite to fight off a common enemy, many Celtic rulers pledged their allegiance to the Romans and became "client kings" as a means of increasing their own power. They signed trade agreements and paid tribute to the Romans, and Caesar was satisfied.

In A.D. 43, as the newly appointed emperor of Rome, Claudius needed a victory to establish his reputation as a strong leader. What could be better than finishing the conquest of Britain, giving him a chance to boast he'd ended what the great Caesar had started? By A.D. 47 most of the southern half of the island was under Roman control. Despite this, Celtic tribes continued to resist during the Roman occupation, especially in the northern half of the island.

Three Ways to Subdue a Nation

Any nation can be conquered if an invader has enough manpower. Making sure a country remains subdued isn't as simple. A conqueror can try to kill off as many people as possible in the conquered country or pacify the country with the advantages of a "superior civilization." The Romans wanted live slaves, not dead bodies, and opted for the second choice.

Stonehenge: A Circle of Standing Stones

At the top of a grassy slope on the Salisbury Plain 30 miles (48 km) north of the English Channel, the Romans discovered a circle of fifty standing stones. Some of the stones weighed 40 tons. The monument was thought to have been built by the Druids, but archaeologists have concluded it was built by an unknown Stone Age people long before the Celts arrived in Britain. Gerald Hawkins, a mathematician from Harvard University, calculated that 1.5 million days of labor—equivalent to approximately 400 years—had been needed to build it using the primitive methods of the era. Scholars debate the purpose of Stonehenge ("hanging stones"). Was it a place of worship or of sacrifice, a giant calendar, or all three?

Agricola Sees a Small Green Island

The Roman general Julius Agricola governed Britain from about A.D. 78 to 84. The Celtic tribes of northern Britain continued to be a problem, but Agricola was victorious in the Battle of Mons Graupius in A.D. 83, during which the Celts used their war chariots for the last time. As the Roman general stood on the Scottish coast, he gazed westward. Approximately 11 miles (18 km) away, a small green island was barely visible through the mist.

The Romans called it Hibernia, and Agricola estimated it could be conquered with a single Roman legion, about 4,000 troops. But why bother? The island was insignificant, isolated on all sides by the sea, and the people who lived on it (rumored to be pygmies or cannibals or both) had no armies. Agricola turned away and gave Hibernia no further thought. The Celts called the island Éire, or Ireland. It would become their last kingdom.

Hadrian's Wall

In A.D. 122, the emperor Hadrian, determined to keep unruly northern Celts out of prosperous southern Britain, built a wall 73 miles (117.5 km) long, 8 feet (2.4 m) thick, and 15 feet (4.6 m) high stretching from England's Tyne River on the east coast to the Solway Firth on the west. Marking each mile of the wall was a "milecastle," or blockhouse that held about twenty soldiers. On the north side was a ditch 27 feet (8.2 m) wide and 9 feet (3 m) deep that further discouraged trespassers. In A.D. 142, a second wall—the Antonine Wall—was built even farther to the north.

The extensive defense system required many troops to maintain. Without adequate manpower, the Romans recruited local men, whose sympathies lay with their countrymen more than with the Romans, to command the lonely outposts. They turned blind eyes when Scottish Celts managed to get over the wall and descend on southern Britain to plunder and murder. Portions of the wall still stand, reminders of a Roman defensive plan that didn't work.

The End of Roman Rule

The mighty Roman Empire eventually fell into decline because of an excess of success. Its armies had conquered vast territories, from Spain in the west to Asia Minor in the east to Britain in the North Atlantic. Administration of such far-flung provinces became increasingly difficult. Corruption among Roman administrators in the provinces weakened the control of the emperor in Rome. At home, Roman citizens grew accustomed to easy wealth and were indifferent to problems faced by the empire.

In 410, a weakened Rome withdrew the last of its troops from southern Britain. By that time, that part of the country had become romanized: British people had adopted Roman customs, rule of law, and the Latin language. They enjoyed the advantages of a Roman lifestyle—city living,

Emperor Hadrian had a massive stone wall built to protect southern Britain from the Celts in the north. Some of the wall still stands today.

public baths, theaters, and fine buildings. They'd also adopted Christianity, a religion brought from Rome. They were more Roman than Celtic and had no desire to be otherwise.

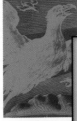

Ireland Before the Celts

Pre-Celtic, Stone Age tribes had settled in small farming settlements in Ireland as early as 4000 B.C. They built elaborate "passage tombs," such as the one at Newgrange, using stones weighing as much as several tons. The structure, dating from about 3100 B.C., was covered with dirt and entered through a narrow opening that faced the rising sun. At dawn on the first day of winter, the sun penetrates a secret chamber deep within the underground vault. When Celtic languages and people evolved in western Europe during the Bronze Age, they incorporated places like Newgrange into their mythology, calling them passageways to the Otherworld.

Persistent Raids

Without a strong Roman presence, Celts raided southern Britain with increasing boldness. Germanic tribes and the Jutes of Denmark also came to pick the bones of the abandoned Roman province. British officials were alarmed, yet realized they couldn't defend their way of life without help. They offered land to the Saxons, a Germanic tribe, in payment for aid in fending off the Celts and others.

The Saxons did indeed come to the rescue of romanized Britain. Then, emboldened by the wealth they saw, they turned on their hosts. The Saxons burned British settlements and killed British citizens, and when they needed reinforcements themselves, they called on another Germanic tribe, the Angles. Together, the Anglo-Saxons seized control of Britain and called it Angle Land—England in modern times.

The victories of the Anglo-Saxons were bad news for the native Celts. Ninety-five percent of the population of Britain lived outside the cities, where romanization proceeded slowly or not at all. Celtic farmers and rural tradespeople clung to their Iron Age customs, the Celtic language, and Druidic beliefs. Under pressure from the Anglo-Saxons, they were pushed into inhospitable western regions of Britain, and farther north into the rough hills of Scotland. Only on the small green island Agricola hadn't thought worth invading did the Celts cling for a few more centuries to their ancient ways.

Myth, Magic, and Irish High Kings

What is known about Celtic life in Ireland has been gathered from Irish stories and myths. Tales of great warrior kings such as Cormac MacAirt, Connor MacNessa, and queens like Maeve of Connacht were handed down from one generation to the next orally, as tales had been handed down among the European Celts.

Irish lore was filled with enchantments, fairies, witches, and with stories of noble heroes such as Cú Chulainn. Because there were no large cities in Ireland, the countryside of meadow and forest was populated by fewer than half a million people who owed their allegiance to various Celtic kings. In Ireland, their last kingdom, the Celts enjoyed what they'd always valued most: freedom to pursue their ancient customs and religion.

Christianity Comes to Ireland

In A.D. 312, Emperor Constantine issued a decree that Christianity would be tolerated, which until this decree was punishable by death. The Catholic faith was adopted by subjects in every corner of the Roman Empire. The romanized Celts of Britain converted, but the Irish Celts continued to worship the ancient "wisdom of the oak." It was the son of a Roman official, Patricius Magonus Sucatus (we call him St. Patrick), who changed their beliefs.

Patrick's Legacy: Monks and Monasteries

Today Patrick is Ireland's patron saint. Men who converted to Patrick's faith sought to imitate his dedication. They renounced the world and retreated to monasteries to devote their lives to prayer and study. They also became skilled copyists of ancient books, illustrating them with elaborate drawings. The most famous is *The Book of Kells*, now on display at Trinity College in Dublin. Monks also did missionary work, converting many others to Christianity, and established schools to educate the children of the faithful. Ordinary Irish folk who'd converted became ***peregrini***, or pilgrims, who set out from their homes to help convert other "pagans" to the Christian faith.

A page from *The Book of Kells*

At age fifteen Patrick was kidnapped as he worked in his father's fields, taken to Ireland, and sold as a slave. He was put to work tending sheep, giving him time to reflect on the religious lessons he hadn't paid attention to in school. Six years later Patrick dreamed that a ship waited for him on the east coast of Ireland. He found it, boarded it, ended up in France, and studied to join the priesthood. A voice in a second dream told Patrick to "come back and walk again among us." He returned to Ireland in about A.D. 450 to spread the Catholic faith. The popular story about Patrick ridding Ireland of snakes isn't true: There never were any snakes on the island.

St. Patrick encouraged people to join his religion, Catholicism.

Invasions and More Invasions

In 795, more than three hundred years after the time of St. Patrick, the Vikings—raiders from Norway—attacked Ireland for the first time. The raiders were attracted by the wealth of Ireland's monasteries, none of which were well defended. They arrived along the coast in their swift, shallow longboats; seized treasure, captives, and livestock; and then departed as swiftly as they'd arrived. As the Vikings' boldness increased, they began to sail inland up Ireland's many rivers. Then in 841, rather than come and go so often, they built a permanent camp along the River Liffey at a place called Dubb Linn.

Persistence of Slavery Among the Celts

Dubb Linn—Dublin as it's known today—became the largest, most important town in Ireland. As the best seaport on the island, it grew wealthy trading cattle, whiskey, and gold and became a major slave market. When Celtic kings waged war against their fellow kings, captives were taken and sold in Dublin to traders from England, Iceland, and Scandinavia.

The Celts drove the Vikings out of Ireland temporarily in 902, but they returned in 914 and settled other towns, such as Waterford, Wexford, Cork, and Limerick. Brian Boru became high king of Ireland in 1001; his victory at the Battle of Clontarf in 1014 put at end to the Viking invasions. But Brian didn't drive the Vikings (now Christian converts themselves) out of the country. He and other Celtic kings understood the commercial advantages of integrating them peacefully into Irish life.

Later, the Celts faced another foe. The Anglo-Norman invasions of Ireland began in 1166 as the result of a quarrel between a Celtic high king, Rory O'Connor, and a low king, Diarmaid MacMurchada. Diarmaid appealed to King Henry II of England for aid. Henry agreed for reasons that had little to do with the desire to help Diamaid. Like the Vikings, the English king was well aware of the riches in Ireland. In 1175, Henry demanded to be recognized as the overlord of Ireland, and by 1603, England dominated all of Ireland. The once-proud Celts, who hated to bend a knee to anyone, became what they'd battled against throughout their long history: mere subjects of a more powerful ruler.

Chapter VIII

CELTS IN THE MODERN WORLD

No country is more closely identified with Celtic heritage than the small, green island Agricola turned his back on in A.D. 84. The majority of the Irish people who live in Ireland today are direct descendants of ancient Celts that once roamed the length and breadth of Europe, who poured down the icy slopes of the Alps to seize the rich farm fields of the Po Valley about 400 B.C.

Only about 20 percent of Ireland is **arable**, or suitable for planting crops. Agriculture, once so important to their Celtic ancestors, now occupies only 8 percent of Irish workers. The rest are employed in industry, which is composed of food processing, the brewing of alcohol, and the manufacturing of textiles, clothing, chemicals, pharmaceuticals, fine crystal, and computer software. Trade is carried on mostly with Britain (41 percent), the United States (15 percent), and Germany (7 percent). Since 1973 Ireland has been a member of the European Union and uses the euro as its currency. Among Ireland's mineral resources are copper, lead, zinc, silver, oil, and natural gas.

While farming was very important to the Celts, only a small percentage of people in Ireland work in agriculture today.

Geologically, Ireland is shaped like a wheel. Ancient volcanic rock forms the rim, and the center is porous limestone. Ten thousand years ago Ice Age glaciers carved the Irish landscape into **eskers** (long ridges) and **drumlins** (low hillocks of soil, rock, and rubble). Grass and flowers blanket these outcroppings, providing homes for a variety of wildlife, including wild goats, deer, and rabbits as well as hunting birds such as peregrine falcons and merlin hawks. Bogs, the soggiest part, dot the middle of the wheel.

The Republic of Ireland is about the size of West Virginia. Twenty-five percent of its 3.9 million citizens live in the capital, Dublin. St. Patrick did his work well, for about 92 percent of the population is Catholic. The official language is English, although Gaelic, the ancient language of the Celts, is taught in public school and is spoken especially along the west coast.

Political Echoes of the Past

Like the ancient Celts under the Romans, modern-day Irish people fought for their independence. The bloody Easter Rebellion of 1916 paved the way for the Irish to reclaim what they'd always loved most: freedom. In 1921, the Irish Free State was established. A new flag—three vertical bands of green, white, and orange—was adopted, and the country's name was changed to the Republic of Ireland. Ireland formally withdrew from the British Commonwealth, and is now divided into twenty-six counties. (Six counties in the northeast corner of the island, called Ulster, remained part of Britain and maintain a capital at Belfast.)

Celtic queens played important roles in ancient Celtic life, and women are no less active in modern Ireland. Mary Robinson was elected president of the Republic of Ireland in 1990. Mary McAleese, the current president, elected in 1997, ran against Mary Banotti. The dream of unifying the island—of bringing Ulster and the Republic together—is a persistent topic of conversation, but to date has not happened.

Presence of the Celts in the Arts and Sports

The ancient Celts were renowned for their storytelling skills. It should be no surprise that the most remarkable impact their Irish descendants have had on the modern world is through literature and poetry. The Celts have been called "wordsmiths"—blacksmiths create works of art out of metal while Irish writers forge works of art out of words. Ireland produced several winners of the Nobel Prize in Literature, including William Butler Yeats (1923), George Bernard Shaw (1925), and Samuel Beckett (1969).

Celtic flutes once urged warriors into battle, and harps were played for the entertainment of kings and nobles. Now Celtic music is enjoyed by people around the world and uses such ordinary but delightful instruments as the pennywhistle. Van Morrison, Sinead O'Connor, James Galway, the Chieftains, the Clancy Brothers—not to mention the popularity of *Riverdance*—have kept alive the ancient Celts' love of music.

Another important part of Celtic culture, horses, remain valued to this day. The ancient Celts rode into history on the backs of sturdy ponies and horses are still an important part of Celtic life. Horse racing, also called steeplechasing, had its beginnings in 1752, when Lord Doneraile hosted a 4.5-mile (7.2-km) race between the church steeples of Buttevant and St. Leger. Sales of Irish racehorses total about $160 million per year. The Dublin Horse Show is the most famous social and sporting event of the summer and attracts people from around the world.

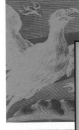

The Mystery of Lindow Man

In August 1984 as two men cut peat at Lindow Moss near Manchester, England, their machine sliced through the bog to a depth of 1 yard (1 m). A piece of wood sticking out of the peat caught their attention. When they examined it more closely, they saw that it was part of a human leg. Had a local resident been murdered and dumped in the bog? The alarmed peat cutters notified the police at once.

Local authorities realized they weren't dealing with an ordinary body. Archaeologists and **forensic** experts (scientists who study crime scenes) were summoned. A few days later the rest of the man's body was located nearby, also preserved in layers of peat. Newspaper and television reporters called the mystery man "Pete Marsh." Investigators respectfully named him "Lindow Man" and asked specific questions as they unraveled his story: Who was Lindow Man? How did he die? When did he die? Why was he left in a peat bog?

Mud and debris were carefully cleaned from the mystery man's body. Scientists discovered he was about twenty-five years old, 5 feet 6 inches (1.7 m) tall, had type-O blood (common to persons of Celtic ancestry), had dark hair, and a neatly trimmed beard. His naked body had been painted with blue dye before death. His fingernails were smooth and clean, indicating he wasn't a farmer or laborer. The **amulet** (charm), or band of fox fur around his upper left arm, suggested he belonged to an elite class. The contents of his stomach revealed that his last meal was of blackened bread sprinkled with mistletoe pollen.

Lindow Man's death had been swift. A heavy blow to the back of his head had crushed his skull and upper vertebrae. A deep knife wound on his neck had severed his carotid artery. What was thought to be a tree root twisted around his neck was in fact a leather rope tied with an unusual knot. Scholars suspect Lindow Man was sacrificed in a Druidic rite called "the three deaths."

The Mystery of Lindow Man (continued)

Two weeks after Lindow Man was found, samples of bone from his hand and leg were examined at the Atomic Energy Research Laboratory at Harwell, England. Carbon dating indicated that he died around 300 B.C., about 2,000 years before the discovery of his body.

Why was he left in a bog? The Celts believed that bodies of water were sacred. Celts named many of the famous rivers of Europe, as well as the Thames ("Dark River") and the Witham ("Forest River") in Britain. The Druids selected watery sites, such as rivers, lakes, and bogs, at which to conduct sacred ceremonies and celebrations—and for ritual sacrifices to guarantee good crops and abundant harvests.

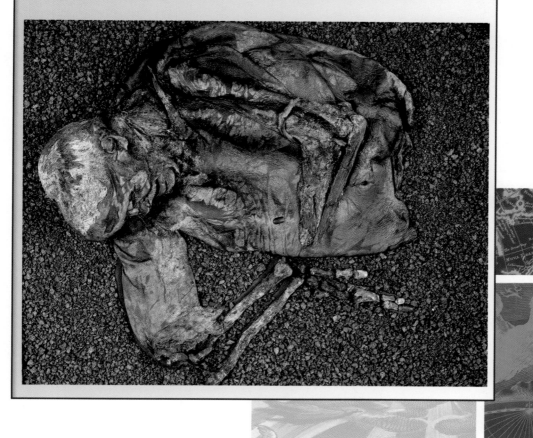

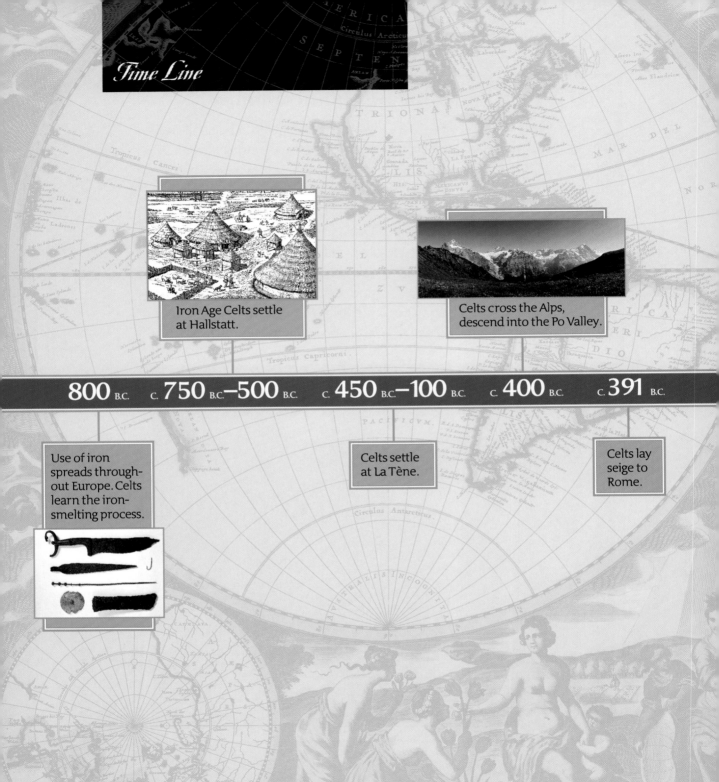

Iron Age Celts settle
at Hallstatt.

Celts cross the Alps,
descend into the Po Valley.

800 B.C.   c. **750** B.C.—**500** B.C.   c. **450** B.C.—**100** B.C.   c. **400** B.C.   c. **391** B.C.

Use of iron
spreads through-
out Europe. Celts
learn the iron-
smelting process.

Celts settle
at La Tène.

Celts lay
seige to
Rome.

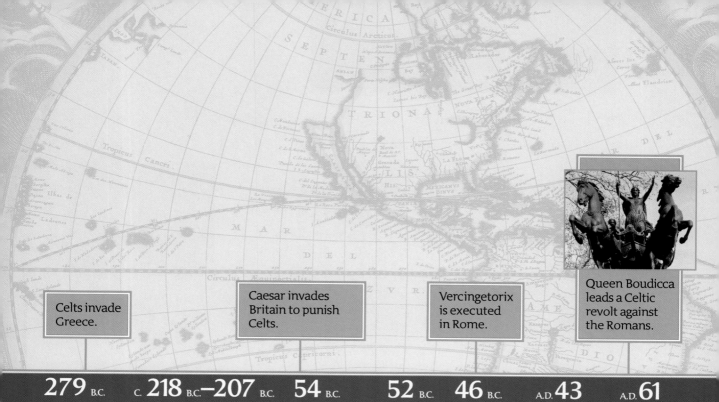

Celts invade Greece.

Caesar invades Britain to punish Celts.

Vercingetorix is executed in Rome.

Queen Boudicca leads a Celtic revolt against the Romans.

| 279 B.C. | c. 218 B.C.–207 B.C. | 54 B.C. | 52 B.C. | 46 B.C. | A.D. 43 | A.D. 61 |

Celtic mercenaries join Hannibal's armies.

Vercingetorix is named the leader of the Celtic tribes in Gaul. Caesar defeats the Celts at Alesia.

Emperor Claudius invades Britain to subdue the Celts.

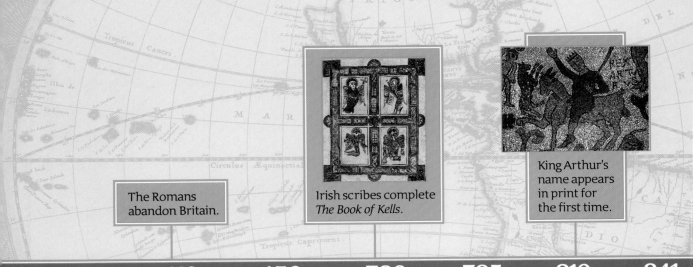

Time Line (continued)

The Romans abandon Britain.

Irish scribes complete *The Book of Kells*.

King Arthur's name appears in print for the first time.

| A.D. **122** | A.D. **410** | C. A.D. **450** | C. A.D. **790** | A.D. **795** | A.D. **810** | A.D. **841** |

Emperor Hadrian builds a stone wall in northern Britain.

St. Patrick converts Irish pagans to Christianity.

The Vikings begin the first of many invasions of Ireland.

City of Dublin is founded by Vikings.

Celts drive the Vikings out of Ireland.

Brian Boru becomes high king of Ireland.

King Henry II of England becomes overlord of Ireland.

Vikings reinvade Ireland and establish the cities of Waterford, Wexford, Cork, and Limerick.

Anglo-Normans invade Ireland.

England completes the domination of Ireland.

A.D. **902**　A.D. **914**　A.D. **1002**　A.D. **1166**　A.D. **1175**　A.D. **1603**

King Arthur

11th–12th century A.D.

King Arthur was most likely a legend, a character based on several different figures from stories and history. The name *Arddu*, "the dark one," was given to a legendary man who battled for the rights of others. Artorius, a warrior-king, fought against the Anglo-Saxon invaders of Britain in early medieval times. Stories about King Arthur were told and retold by so many people that King Henry II claimed to be his real-life descendant when he came to the British throne in 1154.

Boudicca

1st century A.D.

Boudicca became queen of Britain's Iceni tribe when her husband died in A.D. 60. The Romans didn't accept women as lawful rulers and scourged her in public. Boudicca called the Iceni and other Celtic tribes to join her in revolt against the Roman oppressors. She was successful for a time, but was defeated in A.D. 61. Rather than live as a Roman slave, Boudicca took her own life.

Brian Boru

11th century A.D.

Brian Boru became árd rí, or high king of Ireland, in A.D. 1001. At the age of eighty-eight, he was victorious at the Battle of Clontarf in 1014, putting an end to the Viking invasions. He is remembered in Irish history as the mightiest of all Celtic warrior-kings.

Cartimandua

1st century A.D.

Cartimandua, queen of the Brigantes, ruled the largest Celtic kingdom in Britain. Rather than struggle against the Roman invaders as Boudicca did, Cartimandua allied herself with them in A.D. 51. In doing so, she betrayed her husband and her own tribe. The outraged Brigantes drove her into exile. In fear for her life, Cartimandua lived out her days under Roman protection.

Cassivellaunus

1st century B.C.

War-leader Cassivellaunus assumed leadership of the Celtic tribes in southern Britain when the Romans invaded in 54 B.C. He led four thousand charioteers against Caesar's 30,000-man army. The Romans were amazed by the Celts' ability to "control their horses at full gallop . . . and turn them in a moment." In spite of the Celtic charioteers' skill, Cassivellaunus was defeated.

Eochaid Muighmedon

4th century A.D.

Eochaid Muighmedon was a mythical árd rí, or high king, of Ireland about A.D. 350. As the father of five sons, he wished to find out which one would be best able to take the throne when he died. As a test, the king ordered the smithy set afire. Only his son Niall had the good sense to carry the blacksmith's tools to safety. It was he who became king at his father's death.

Nuada of the Silver Hand

12th century A.D.

King Nuada of medieval Irish legend knew that a Celtic king needed to be perfect, a man without flaw in body or spirit. When he lost a hand in battle, he quickly ordered a new hand made out of silver, complete with movable fingers and joints. His tribespeople weren't convinced it made him perfect enough. King Nuada was forced to step aside for a fitter man.

Princess of Vix

C. 500 B.C.

The Princess of Vix got her name after archaeologists discovered a burial chamber at Vix, near Burgundy, France, in 1953. Inside the chamber were the remains of a Celtic woman who had been laid to rest in about 500 B.C. She wore a gold torque, a shroud made of leather rather than of common linen, and was surrounded by fine objects for her journey to the next world. Although her rank can't be known with certainty, the rich goods in her burial chamber indicate that she was a person of royal birth.

Vercingetorix

1st century B.C.

King Vercingetorix of the Arverni tribe was the first warrior-king to unite other Celts under the leadership of a single chieftain. He led his combined forces into battle against Caesar's armies, but was defeated at Alesia in 52 B.C. The Romans held Vercingetorix captive for six years, then executed him in 46 B.C.

Glossary

airechta   warrior who took a would-be king's place in combat

amber   fossilized tree resin

amphorae   clay wine container

amulet   good-luck charm

arable   suitable for agriculture

ard   simple wooden plow

Arddu   possible origin of King Arthur's name

árd rí   high king

Beltane   festival celebrating the beginning of summer, May 1

booleying   moving livestock to open pasture

branduh   "black raven"; Celtic board game

cannabis   marijuana; member of nettle family

Celtae   Roman translation of the Greek word *keltoi*

daub   clay or mud mixed with straw

dru   oak tree

drumlin   low hillock

Drunemeton   oak sanctuary

einkorn   ancient variety of wheat

emmer   ancient variety of wheat

esker   long ridge

Feis Temhra   Feast of Tara

fidchell   "wooden wisdom"; board game similar to chess

filidh   bard, storyteller

fir fer   fair play

forensics   scientific study of crime scenes

fosterage Celtic practice of placing their children in the homes of other families

freeman tenant farmer

haggis a type of Scottish food

himbas forosnai foresight, gift of prophecy

Imbolc festival celebrating the beginning of spring, February 1

Keltoi "secret" people, Greek name for Celts

krater Greek wine vessel

Lia Fail Stone of Destiny in Ireland

Lughnasadh festival celebrating the beginning of autumn, August 1

magistri sapientica "masters of wisdom"

mead wine made from honey

moldboard curved blade on a plow

murex shellfish that produces purple dye

peat carbonized leaves, grass; used as fuel

peregrini Irish pilgrims

preliterate culture with no written language

rath ancient enclosure

ruan herb used to redden women's cheeks

Salzkammergut "salt roads"

Samhain festival celebrating the beginning of winter, October 31 or November 1

sheep's pluck sheep's heart, lung, liver

spelt ancient variety of wheat

táin cattle raid

Tara site where Irish kings were crowned

Tir na n-Og "Land of Youth"

torque neck ring

túath tribe

turf peat

umbo hand grip on a Celtic shield

wattle wall made of branches

woad plant that produces blue dye

BOOKS

Hinds, Kathryn. *The Celts of Northern Europe*. Tarrytown, NY: Benchmark Books, 1997

Martell, Hazel Mary. *The Celts*. New York: Viking, 1996.

Martell, Hazel Mary. *What Do We Know About the Celts?* New York: Peter Bedrick Books, 1999.

Lassieur, Allison. *The Celts*. San Diego: Lucent Books, 2001.

ORGANIZATIONS AND ONLINE SITES

Celtic Culture
http://www.georgetown.edu/labyrinth/subjects/british_isles/celtic/celtic.html

This site, created by Georgetown University, provides access to electronic resources in Celtic studies, including primary sources, databases, and more.

Encyclopaedia of the Celts
http://celt.net/Celtic/celtopedia/indices/encycintro.html

This is the online version of "The Encyclopaedia of the Celts" and contains a wealth of information on the Celts, including mythological and historic figures, chronicles, sites, events, magic rituals, folklore, and their reflection in literature.

Encyclopedia Mythica
http://www.pantheon.org/

This site has more than 4,000 entries on gods, legendary figures, other supernatural beings, and imaginary places from a variety of cultures and civilizations.

Ethnologue, Web Version
http://www.ethnologue.com/web.asp

Learn more about Celtic language from this classification database of the world's living and recently extinct languages.

Internet Medieval Sourcebook: The Celtic World
http://www.fordham.edu/halsall/sbook1g.html

Visitors to this site will find a collection of primary text resources on the medieval history and culture of the Celtic world.

Irish History on the Web
http://larkspirit.com/history/

This Web site contains information on the history and prehistory of Ireland, with particular attention to the modern period. It includes genealogy and literature resources, time lines, and lists of universities offering Irish studies.

Patricia Calvert grew up in Montana, whose meadows, hills, and valleys are as beautiful as those described in Celtic legends. She lived in the woods near Big Timber Creek, climbed hills with names like Thunder Mountain, the Long Hill, and Old Baldy. She had dogs, cats, horses—even a brother named John. Patricia's great-grandparents on her father's side of the family were Scottish Celts; on her mother's side they were Irish Celts. When Patricia grew up, she traveled to the lands her ancestors came from. She hiked the Highlands beyond Hadrian's Wall, walked the streets of Dublin along the River Liffey, and imagined what life had been like in Celtic days of long ago.